BITCOIN

The Brief Guide To Investing In Bitcoin With Practical Tips And Tricks

Adrian McNulty

© Copyright 2018 by Adrian McNulty - All rights reserved.

It is not legal to reproduce, duplicate, or transmit any part of this document in either electronic means or in printed format. Recording of this publication is strictly prohibited.

Table Of Contents

Introduction 7

Chapter 1: How Bitcoin Works 15

Chapter 2: Basics Of Investing And Trading Bitcoin 32

Chapter 3: Should You Mine In A Pool Or Solo 42

Chapter 4: How To Set Up A Bitcoin Miner 60

Chapter 5: The Network Of Bitcoin 70

Chapter 6: Strategies To Use In Mining And Trading Bitcoin 86

Conclusion 98

Introduction

Bitcoin is a decentralized payment system that was launched as a currency in the year 2009 by Satoshi Nakamoto. It is the most popular and the latest outcome of practical efforts of creating a digital currency. Initially bitcoin issue was 2,625,000, which improved to 12,091, 050 by 7, December 2013. By then, the value of each bitcoin was $736.61. Bitcoin is a virtual form of currency whose operations are software based. This form of money is completely electronic.

Mining, Trading And Investing In Bitcoin

The proliferation and growth of digital transactions has brought about borderless exchange systems for electronic trading and investing. Today, the traditional currency is less preferred as most people have diverted to use of cryptocurrency. Bitcoin mining, investing and trading is unique and new economic activity that the world has never seen before. Bitcoin is an international currency allowing a globalized economy. This currency is decentralized and independent of central bank or any country control.

Bitcoin is an international currency that has fascinated many worldwide investors and traders. These includes business executives, anti-government and government advocates, and computer experts among others. Bitcoin currency provides anonymity to its holders, inflation protection, and protection from insecurity, fraud and theft. This currency concept has enabled cash and cash equivalent valuables to be used globally over the internet hence expounding and boosting the economy internationally.

Mining Bitcoins Successfully

The profitability in bitcoin mining is solely dependent on the miner's willingness to spend. Understanding mining profitability calculators provides in-depth knowledge on how much a miner should expect after undertaking the mining activity. The profits generated by different miners varies depending on the applicability of the mining requirements. Such parameters as hardware cost and electricity cost among other variables are key factors. These determine the extent of projection of profit generated by different members.

Trading And Investing In Bitcoin

Bitcoin is the fastest, more secure and more affordable fund transfer option. Technically, bitcoin is a digital currency that is math-based. It is open sourced, finite and verifiable. This is a decentralized virtual and electronic currency which relies on cryptography for enhanced security.

Bitcoin traders and investors work to solve "double spending problem" which is so prominent with other form of digital goods. Double spending means copying and using the same information repeatedly. Unlimited copying possibility for digital currency, would lead to a sudden hyperinflationary death. Bitcoin ensures this problem is solved by maintaining a network of peer to peer and keeping a recording of each transaction on bitcoin block chains also known as public ledgers.

Therefore, if a trader sends a bitcoin from their bitcoin address to a trading partner, that bitcoin is recorded by the network in a transaction blockchain. The possession changes from the trader to the trading partner immediately it has moved from the traders wallets to their trading partner's wallet. The traders and potential investors have greatly benefited from the use of this new payment form of digital phenomenon.

Decentralization Of Bitcoin

Bitcoin works as a decentralized currency, whereby the peer to peer transaction is carried without involving any middlemen. Therefore, the activities of the peers are not under control the central authority or any other middle persons. Traders and bitcoin investors can freely transact with anyone in the entire world, with any bitcoin amount. Unlike the traditional methods where third parties must be involved, bitcoin exchange system is completely independent. Banks and other forms of money transmitters are never share takers here. More so, this cryptocurrency freely allows AML restrictions and capital bypassing.

Internet and the bitcoin wallet address are the key requirement for someone to engage in trading, mining and investing in bitcoins. Additionally, one should ensure that they are online adequately to give time for the processing of the transactions. Just as the traditional banking systems, a bitcoin accounts holder is able to receive bitcoins in their bitcoin address, while online as well as when offline. However internet connections is a necessary requirement as one can easily collect their coins, trade and invest effectively.

Understanding Bitcoin Mining Variables

Hash Rate

This refers to the number of calculations you make in every second. The number of calculations made is purely dependent on the efficiency and effectiveness of the miner. This means that the more calculations you need, the more effective your miner should be. Your miner is also known as the horse power and the only mining variable that you have control over.

Bitcoin Mining Difficulty

Bitcoin mining difficulty denotes the level of hardness involved in creating/ finding a bitcoin block. The measure of hardness rises as the price of bitcoin increases. This is however adjusted within a duration of two weeks. Sometimes, you will realize that the level difficulty is too high, beyond the bitcoin value. Well, though you have cannot control the difficulty level, you need to note that it has control a very direct impact to profit addition.

Pool Cut

While joining the mining industry, it is important to remember that you can either solo mine; mine alone, or pool mine; mine with other miners. Mostly, solo mining is less profitable as compared to pool mining. It is therefore advisable to pool mine. There are many pool miners out there, all you need is to choose and join the best and largest pools. . Normally, the greatest advantage with pools is that they share in your losses as they share in your gains. However, they only take a very small cut from the bitcoins you mine. Most mining pools have static mining fees. Here, you can control this in the fact that you can choose your preferable mining pool.

Bitcoin Price

Bitcoin miners get bitcoins as rewards for undertaking the mining. Though it may fluctuate, the overall trend of the price is always going upwards. Note that the payout value is directly proportional to the value of bitcoin. This means that an increase in bitcoins value leads to an increase in payout. No one has control over payout or the value of bitcoins; the strangeness and market volatility deals with this.

Most investors and trading businessmen make abnormal profits from bitcoins by waiting for their price to rise. Bitcoins can also be exchanged to dollars through selling them to exchange systems like the Coinbase. Remember to use such sites as Coinwarz, to check your math's and determine the overview of you profit.

Understanding How To Trade With Bitcoins

Using Bitcoin requires one to have all the basic information cutting across any knowledge regarding its use. Well, this is explained in this book to ensure that your Bitcoins are secure and you are at peace with your mining, trading and investing. Internalizing the various explained aspects of this book will give you a full explanation concerning: winning brand new Bitcoin awards, using your Bitcoins among other. All you will require considering before taking any further step is **to have a bitcoin secured wallet**. A wallet is your bank, which should be well guarded and secured, else you may lose everything. Among the Bitcoins wallets available to choose from include: mobile Bitcoin wallet, hardware-based wallet and the web-based wallet. Mostly some will back up there secured web-based wallets to ensure that computer hackers do not get access to their savings.

Chapter 1: How Bitcoin Works

How bitcoin works is not anonymous as everyone expected. Detailed information are discussed below to provide an in-depth insight for a more simplified approach and understanding on how to work and earn with bitcoin.

Fundamentally, bitcoin currency works as a secured system through which internet money is stored and exchanged anonymously. It is important to understand the anonymity involved in working with bitcoin even before finding out various fields where use of bitcoin is applicable. This requires you to dig on understanding: how to own the bitcoins, trading tactics as well as secure methods of using this digital currency.

Understanding How Bitcoin Works

This is the most interesting, yet the basic requirement for bitcoin users, traders and the investors. The discussion below provides simple basics in the most simplified manner which you must keenly master to work effectively and efficiently with bitcoins. You should therefore:

1. Start By Owning A Bitcoin Digital Wallet

In order to understand how to own bitcoin, someone should start by understanding how to get a bitcoin digital wallet. This is a place for stashing bitcoins in the future. Once you have acquired a digital wallet, you can store your bitcoins there as well as receive and send bitcoins.

The blockchain. Info and the coinbase are two examples of the internet based services where you can get your own digital wallet. After owning a digital wallet, you can be sure that your bitcoins are safe and secure against breach. All the digital wallets are available on mobile apps for those using the androids. Those storing their bitcoins locally in a computer hard drive should consider downloading a desktop digital wallet app. A good example is the MultiBit desktop digital wallet. The only thing that you should remember here, is to back up your app, regularly and ensure that your computer is safe and secure.

A blockchain info. Digital wallet service enables the user to establish more than one bitcoin addresses. Each address gives you a chance to send or receive bitcoins from other bitcoin owners. Just like an email, people should not know beyond your address in order to send you the bitcoins. The addresses are usually convoluted and long as the real world will not need them beyond their necessity of sending the bitcoins.

2. Fill Your Wallet With Bitcoins

As soon as you have a digital wallet, the next step is to fill them with bitcoins. Depending on the ability of the buyer, bitcoin are available in whole blocks or as fractions. This is because bitcoins are not cheap.

Best Options To Get Your Own Bitcoins

While deciding on where and how to own your bitcoins, it is important to go for the less anonymous option to avoid complications that would lead to future loses. Moreover, use an option that is common; one that most people have used and found the best. Below are some of options that will help you land to your own bitcoins easily and securely.

- Buying from bitcoin exchange

- Mining bitcoins

- Buying from a nearby trader or a friend

- Accepting them as payment value in exchange to goods or services you have provided

Origin Of Bitcoin Addresses

Unlike other coins, bitcoins coins are known to have features that are not fully anonymous. Bitcoin addresses is a feature that was added by the developers as they sought to solve anonymity shortcomings of bitcoins as its anonymity is not fully anonymous like the other crypto coins. Such coins have also been developed with additional features that are lacking in other types of coins, hence are thought to be more anonymous. Besides being invented to compliment the less anonymous bitcoin, bitcoin address play a greater role in completing transaction among the transacting parties.

Creation Of Bitcoin Addresses

Bitcoin addresses can either be downloaded or gotten from online wallets. Multibit and the Bitcoin-qt are the most common client addresses. The two differ due to the difference in the block size being downloaded. For the Bitcoin-qt, your hard drive requires a free space of at least 10 Gigabytes to accommodate the block chain.

How Bitcoin Addresses Operate

The bitcoin system will add transfer details. Total bitcoins are being transferred among the addresses of the parties transacting as soon as a bitcoin transfer command is made. The system record will indicate additional entry to the receiving address and subtraction entry to the sending address immediately the transaction as taken place. The information on the past events and the transaction taking place are recorded on a public, which remains there permanently.

Bitcoin Addresses Serving As Identifiers

Bitcoin address is created to function like an email address. The similarity is that, this address can be shared just like the email address so that a trading partner can send you coins. The only difference between the bitcoin address and the email address is that, tough a trader can have many bitcoin addresses, they are recommended to have a major and a unique address involving every transaction undertaken.

Bitcoin addresses serve as identifiers for use while carrying out peer-peer transactions. Therefore, a bitcoin address an alphanumeric identifier of the 26-35 characters that are being identified. These characters begin with numbers used to represent possible bitcoin payment destination. These could be characters beginning with number 1 or the number 3. Creating a bitcoin address is free and simple. Every person undertaking a bitcoin transaction therefore can freely and simply generate an address by clicking an option "new address" on the Bitcoin core. Bitcoin addresses are also available for the users using the online wallet services or the exchanges accounts.

Green Address Bitcoin Wallet

This is a bitcoin wallet that operates by use of addresses among those transacting. With the use the green address Green, the user can easily access his/her bitcoins using different types of methods. Such include: through a client desktop, a mobile app and using online services. This is regarded as the most user friendly and flexible wallet. With its ability to Supports multi-signature features, the green address has privacy features and it uses a strong security.

Such addresses were specifically invented to make use of bitcoins an easy activity among the newbies as they are simple to understand, easier to use and flexible. However, the bitcoin address users require use of remote apps that are loaded from specific location. The address owner will therefore need to share their control over their Bitcoins with the third party for approval of payments.

Bitcoin Transactions

Bitcoin transaction can be defined as value transfer among wallets which is added in the block chain thereafter. A private seed also known as private key is a piece of data that is secretly kept in a user's wallet. This data is used in signing the undertaken transactions. After signing, the private key or the seed will also provide a mathematical evidence or proof that this data has come from the wallet of the user. Upon signing, the owner is sure that this signature will hinder any kind of alterations that may be done by unauthorized user after it is issued. The transaction carried by the users are used broadcasts, which begin network confirmation through undertaking the mining process.

Understanding Bitcoin Traceability

All bitcoins transactions are carried out in a traceable and a public manner upon which they are stored in a bitcoin network permanently. Dealing with bitcoin transactions is a challenge among most users. This is due to the high level transparency level that is not common in the normal traditional transactions.

Bitcoin address is used as the only way providing information on details regarding the sender and the receiver of the bitcoins. Once a transaction has taken place, the bitcoin address is created in the user's wallet. These addresses are permanently tainted as part of the history of the previous transactions they are involved with. All the users participating in a particular transaction can view the balances of every user, all addresses as well as their history of transactions. So that a user can receive goods or services, he/she has to reveal their bitcoin addresses as a form of identity hence the bitcoin address will never be fully anonymous.

Due to the permanency state of the block chain, the user should note that something untraceable currently is bound to become trivial and traceable in the near future. Therefore, bitcoin users should consider using their addresses just once and avoid disclosing such addresses for the safety of their bitcoins

Bitcoin Transaction Network

Bitcoin transactions rotate along individuals, hence a networking process. Well, different transactions operate in different networking model. There are the peer to peer transactions outlining the peer addresses and indicating the source and destination of every transaction. Every single transaction has two destinations and two or more addresses. The first destination is the peer partner where you are transferring your Bitcoins. The second destination is represented by the address of the user wallet, while the third destination is not determined by either of the two peers. It represents the address of the intermediary arising in the transaction especially when the destinations of the two transacting peers did not add up.

This is a scenario where the third destination is introduced. Ann and Betty are carrying out a Bitcoin transaction where Ann sent 100 Bitcoins to Betty. For this case, Betty address is our first destination while Ann's user wallet address where the 100 Bitcoins are being charged represents the second destination. A situation may arise where Isaac address shares the same wallet with Ann. In such a circumstance, the three destination will contain the following Bitcoins in their addresses: Ann address 150 Bitcoins, betty address 100 Bitcoins and Isaac address 49.5 Bitcoins. The missing 0.5 Bitcoins represents transaction fee payment to the miners. Once the mining activity is over, it is encrypted for network submission and continuity of the next step which is confirmation. This occurs when the network takes the encrypted transaction and it is added to the already existing block. It is only after the transaction has been fully encrypted in the current block chain when Betty is able to claim the 100 Bitcoins sent by Ann as his own.

Bitcoin- QT is the software installed in the device of the transacting peers. With it the user wallet is safe and secure in their devices. The software moreover creates a peer to peer network node that helps in block chain distribution. This node signals a working command hence mining starts once the node is used to register a miner. The two peers can now make a request to start mining. The lottery won during mining help in boosting the processing power of the network. After every mining activity the miners get hash as a form of payment.

Confirmation Of A Bitcoin Transactions
The transaction is confirmed as soon as it has been included permanently on a block chain. The main

concept here however is that "permanently included" is not an absolute notion. Therefore the community simply considers a reasonably safe policy, whereby transactions confirmed are considered to be "included with very high probability." The time it takes for a transaction to be confirmed is variable. Some may take tens of minutes and sometimes two or more hours. However, the average time is estimated to be about an hour.

Working Of Block Chains

Since the introduction of internet in marketing, block chains technology has been ranked the best invention. Through this technology, value exchange is done trust free and without central authority involvement.

Block chain technology uses codes, a block chain running program where transactions are transferred automatically. The system is designed in a manner that trust is not necessary and that coding and special mathematical function are used to provide reliability and security.

How Bitcoin Block Chain Works

The chain starts with someone requesting a transaction. The requested transaction is broadcast to peer to peer network consisting of networks known as the nodes. The network of nodes validates the transaction and the users' status using known algorithms. A verified transaction involves cryptocurrency, contracts, and records among other information.

Once verified, the transaction is combined with other transactions hence creating a new block of data for ledger. This new block of data is added to the existing block chain in a permanent and unalterable manner, hence completing the transaction.

The complete transaction acts as a public ledger forming a block chain, which forms the foundation of the entire bitcoin network. The chronological order and the integrity of the blockchain is reinforced with cryptography. Every transaction included in a block chain is confirmed enabling bitcoin wallet users to make calculations of their balance for further spending. Once a transaction is verified, it is also included in the bitcoin wallet to be part of the spenders' spendable bitcoins. Therefore, block chain is created from a log of both existing and new transactions that have been verified to be part of Bitcoin network.

Exploring Bitcoin Networking Blocks

To explore block chain, one should be able to fully understand the hash function and how it operates. Well, hash function is defined as a mathematical process taking input data made of various sizes, performing the required an operation, and returning output data with a fixed size. Hash function is commonly used for passwords storing.

Therefore, when someone creates a web service account operating by use of a password, the hash function digest the password hash message and stores it. Any time you log in to your account, the entered word password, the hash function runs on it to establish if it matches with stored digested message.

Note that, after every mining activity a hash is produced. In case the hash produced as a lower value compared to the block found previously, then, a new Bitcoin block has been discovered which should then be passed for submission and verification. The P2P network have also to confirm the new found block to allow for the closing of the old block and opening of the newly discovered block. Thereafter the founder of the block is awarded.

Well, a transaction shall be considered confirmed in case the P2P network has attained a total of six transaction confirms achieved by creation of new blocks. Confirmation play a vital role in ensuring that double spending does not occur during a transaction.

Can Bitcoin Be Created Out Of Thin Air?

Investing and trading Bitcoin seems like creating money out thin air. This is because, with a good understanding on how to trade with bitcoins, the return prospects is very high. Bitcoin has great value and its real; it is the first ever decentralized digital currency and a worldwide payment system.

As a matter of fact, money is not necessarily the real value for bitcoins. Instead, Bitcoin's value is based on mathematical equations used to solve the counterfeit information problem. Bitcoins are produced as a means of payment to the bitcoin miners. This is exchanged to flat currencies for use in other operations.

Creation of a bitcoins through the mining is a process that requires inputs just like any other activities payable using other flat currencies. Bitcoin mining is a real minting activity; not fake as assumed. The process is fully verifiable by network before being confirmed as 100% authentic. According to reviews from most miners, duplication and counterfeiting digital information of bitcoins is the most difficulty thing to do in the world. It would be much easier for me to counterfeit your Passport, car title, house title and $1,000,000 cash than it is to counterfeit even .00000001 Bitcoin.

Understanding bitcoin mining and the blockchain technology requires the miner to invest in hardware that will, support their block chain network. Bitcoin is rewarded to the successful creators of a new block. It is therefore very vital to work hard in understanding the core block chain systems as the bitcoin mining fundamentals.

Creating a decentralized and trusted network requires great knowledge on bitcoin protocol and the blockchain architecture. What this does is that they take away power from a central trusted body and share it among the network stakeholders. Today the Federal Reserve of equivalent in every nation "generates money out of thin air" by printing notes and coins. The Bitcoin (and others altcoins like Litecoin, Ethereum etc.) simply do the same. The difference is they take away control from a trusted body and decentralize it.

Chapter 2: Basics Of Investing And Trading Bitcoin

After understanding how bitcoin works, investing in it becomes simpler. More a bitcoin investor requires knowledge on how to differentiate bitcoin with fiat currency as well as how to keep their bitcoins secured.

To invest in bitcoins, one should start by buying some. The easiness of buying a bitcoin is dependent on the buyer's country. By so saying, I mean that it is easier buying in developed than developing countries as the developed countries have more liquidity and more options as compared to the developing countries.

A potential buyer would be advised to consider Coinbase bitcoin broker. These is the most prominent and largest broker able to operate to a wider region. They are available in most of the European countries, UK, United States, Singapore and Canada. In case one does not live in any of the mentioned countries, then they can consider buying using an exchanger finder.

Coinbase is an internationally recognized digital wallet allowing investors to buy Bitcoins securely, use them effectively as well as accept the bitcoin currency.

Investing Using A Coinbase Wallet

Coinbase wallet makes transfer of payment easier and faster. Using the coin base, one is required to link their bank account using the coin base link option. You can also make automatic buying using the coin base regular interval buying offer. What you do is you setup a monthly or a weekly auto-buy of a certain amount on Coinbase depending on your preferable interval. Once you get to that interval, you will automatically buy the bitcoins for the amount set on Coinbase.

While investing, it is important to consider some caveats before starting to use the auto-buy services. Note that once one has issued the auto-buy order, the price of the bitcoins is beyond their control. Hence charges shall be done depending on the present bitcoin buying rate. Besides, it is important to know that there may be delays while buying bitcoins on the Coinbase. This is simply because, it does not do bitcoin exchange;

in fact, what you do is that you buy/sell your coins from the firm directly, after being sourced them from various buyers. This is associated with such problems as delay issues especially when orders are being executed on a fast move market periods.

Buying Bitcoins The Traditional Way

BitStamp wallet is the best option for those traders in need of a traditional exchange method for the bitcoins. This gives you a chance to trade with the rest of the bitcoin users, unlike other method where you are required to trade with a company as your middlemen. The method is preferred by most people as it offers a higher liquidity. Moreover, this is best way one can get to interact with other users and may be cross to the trading side. BiStamp offers affordable and customer friendly charges. Those that have traded with over $150,000within a period of 30 days are charged as low as 0.2%, while the beginners fee is 0.5%.

Other Ways To Buy Bitcoins

Local bitcoins is a well-known method through which investors buy bitcoins offline. Therefore you can use it as an alternative in case the online exchange method do not suit you. Local bitcoins, pair up both the potential sellers and the buyers. During the buying process, the bitcoins in the escrow are locked from being accessed by the seller. The seller is only able to release the bought bitcoins to the buyer. A dispute should be filed after a period of 24 hours in case a problem arises after buying the bitcoins. For your security when buying bitcoins offline, it is advisable to do so during the day and in a safe place. However, it could be wise to avoid buying bitcoins from strangers when using the offline method

Bitcoins are also available in such auction sites as the eBay among others. On the eBay auction site, bitcoins are availed for trade on premium to avoid fraud problems and chargeback possibilities.

Some of the bitcoin traders you may meet are willing to do a face meetup. You can visit the localbitcoins.com to meet with the local bitcoin sellers near your place. As reminder, practice safety by ensuring that you meet people in open places and during the day when using the offline method.

Making the choice on how and where purchase bitcoins should be made basing on very wise, calculative and informed decision. Therefore, your requirements should form the basis for your decision. Different exchanges have different options depending on their line of trade. Some exchange options have withdrawal options, bank wire deposit options as well as super banking relations.

Bitcoin Trading

Today Bitcoin is being used extensively in almost every trading ground. Bitcoin currency is being used as untraceable money or a method of depositing money safely without a bank. The use of this currency is so rampant among the dark net traders; who avoid being traced. Bitcoin is widely being used by people who want to keep away from the government prying eyes as no banks is involved when handling this form of money. Notably, bitcoin is more common among the traders; used as a bond or a stock or a tradable financial asset

BTC-E is the easiest exchange to use for the forex traders interested in bitcoin trading. BTC-E company provides a trading platform; MetaTrader for use by its clients. This instrument is excellent in bitcoin shorting due to the 3 to 1 leverage features. Those using the BitStamp do not have the shorting option. With the BitStamp, it is possible to sell the bitcoins you own at any exchanges but outright shorting of bitcoin is impossible.

MetaTrader charging fees are a bit higher compared to those of the BTC-E web interface. There charges 0.3% each side, while the BTC-E charges 0.2%. For the forex traders BTC-E stands to be the best among the discussed three options.

Ownership of the BTC-E is not known by anyone. The company headquarters are apparently situated in Bulgaria. The support staff are fluent in Russian than with English. The depositing and the withdrawal operations of the company remains complicated and a mystery to many. They do so by relaying money through payment processors and several banks before they are finally deposited to the intended account. While planning to deposit through BTC-E, ensure you keenly follow the rules regarding their depositing requirements. Note that your deposits will go through many bank webs hence tracking them down in case of a loss is impossible.

The greatest advantage of trading your bitcoins with BTC-E is that it offers several withdrawal and deposit offers. These include several and popular e-wallets such as the Ukash, Webmoney, Paypal and the PerfectMoney. Both withdrawals work at a minimum of $500 only. The withdrawals and deposits made using these methods are smoother and faster than the bank wires. However, BTC-E do not accept clients from US, any dollar wires from US or US connected bank wires.

On daily basis, forex currency pairs can only move 1% while the bitcoin prices is known to fall or rise by 30% or more within a day. A person well versed in trading may not necessarily need to use a leverage in order to earn through bitcoin trading.

Leveraged Bitcoin Trading Options

As discussed earlier, BTC)- E stands out to be the most competitive option with leveraging and bitcoin shorting advantages. Bulgarian exchange option is known due to the MetaTrader platform; with 3-1 leverage 0.3% low fee on every side and the bitcoin shorting abilities.

Bitcoin Trading With The Ava Trade Option

This is common among the bitcoin forex brokers which uses the CFD for bitcoin trading. The available CFDs are the Bitcoin weekly and the Bitcoin mini. Bitcoin Weekly CFD has a leverage of 20 - 1 leverage expiring at 21:00 GMT on every Friday. On the other hand, Bitcoin Mini offers only 2- 1 leverage without expiring. Both weekly and the mini CFDs use BTC-E data and AVA Trade data adding to around 10$ premium above the set exchange spread.

Bitcoin Trading Addresses

Bitcoin addresses are developed after every transaction. Though the bitcoin addresses are not linked to any private information of the user, Bitcoin ledger can be viewed by anyone using the bitcoin addresses to trace the flow of the funding in every transaction. This is not possible while trading with other coins as they are developed with full anonymity.

The major drawback affecting the two CFDs is their inability to carry out weekend trading. Contrary to this bitcoin trading is set open on 24/7b basis. This is because it is completely decentralized, hence doesn't require any banking network to execute the trading time frame.

Bitcoin Trading With Etoro.com Option

This is one of the latest forex broker with bitcoin trading services. Unlike other trading options, Etoro allows entry and exit to the market only 4 times on daily basis. Therefore, it is gauged as unsuitable for the day traders. According to Etoro bitcoin trading option, the price referencing is the BitStamp's data.

Btc.sx exchange trading option allows traders depositing bitcoins only and not fiat currency. Its leverage product ranges between 10-1 leverage and it's based on BitStamp's data feed. Ava Trade and Btc.sx adds at least 10$ to BitStamp exchange spread. Therefore to trade at Btc.sx, one will need to deposit at least 0.01033 bitcoin for trade to take place. According to the current bitcoin pricing, $638, this is equivalent to approximately 6.3$. Btc.sx, incorporated dually in Singapore and England.

Investing in bitcoins is a tricky yet a simple undertaking. It is therefore important to understand dangers of potential pitfalls while dealing with the bitcoins and the best storage practices to avoid losing the coins as soon as you start owning them. Be careful and keen on your proceedings and avoid anything that might cause melt down of your bitcoins causing you to lose everything.

Chapter 3: Should You Mine In A Pool Or Solo

Theoretically speaking, when you have zero percent pool fee; solo mining and pool mining tend to produce the same revenue in the long run. Most pools keep the transaction fees, consequently making this the only exception. Therefore, mining in a pool or solo is completely dependent on the pool fee.

When it comes to solo mining, take the case that you earn 5 Bitcoin per day; this will result to 50 Bitcoin blocks in 10 days although this is random. You might end up mining two blocks in a day or even not getting any blocks in three or so weeks. When the struggle changes, the amount you are paid changes plus the time between payments drastically change.

In pool mining, the fee is taken right off the top. When you have a 5% pool fee, this means that you will make 5% less. Pools do not pay for the transaction fee, but you have more predictable revenue. You will be paid on regular basis and have payments that don't vary a lot.

Solo mining is more reliable, as you are not dependent on other people's system for your mining to keep going. This is possible in solo mining when you have a mining proxy with a "fallback pool" configuration. For pools, outages and denial of service attacks are the problem.

It is recommended that you use solo mine if you have enough hash power; in order to be able to generate at least one block in a day. In the case where you have a lesser hash power use pool mine. This is a better alternative to the possibility of being unlucky by not getting a block.

How To Solo Mine

Solo mining is where the miner does the task of mining operations alone. The blocks generated and mined are completed by the miner's credit. This process is done without having to join other miners.

When it comes to solo mining, ensure that you connect your miner to your local Bitcoin client. This increases your chances of finding your own block. Although, the probability tends to decrease you will not share your block incentive.

Install the Bitcoin-core; this is a hardware that is used in solo mining. Then create a Bitcoin.conf file: C:\User\yourusername\AppData\Roaming\Bitcoin\

Use 127.0.0.1:8332 as the server, username and for passwords choose the credentials required; in connecting BFGMiner or CGMiner to Bitcoin-core client to have it mined.

How It Works
1. Assuming you are on win x
2. Download the qt wallet
3. Synch up the blockchain
4. Close the client and find the file folder C:\computer\root\user\xxx\AppData\Roaming\Yourcoin

Here 'C' is the local drive

Root is the LocalDriveC

xxx is your name or your log in on the system

Yourcoin is the name of your coin

5. In the folder make new text file with the following.

server=1

listen=1

daemon=1

rpcuser=x

rpcpassword=q

rpcallowip=localhost

rpcport=y

port=z

here X is your name

p is your password

y is the rpc port the coin uses

z is the communication port the network uses

The rpcport on most coins can be set to anything; but the coins do not work in this manner. The port line, daemon and listen lines can be left out, although including these lines increases your chances of getting a solid connection to the network.

In the case where the coin ANN thread or the description has any list of nodes, make a line for each and add the ones like the following:

addnode=h.h.h.h

addnode=j.j.j.j

the h and j are the octets of an IP address; at times the domain can be used.

6. Rename the file Yourcoin.conf

The upper and lower case does not matter in windows, when naming your conf file; but spelling of the coin correctly matters a lot. Save it in form of read only file then restart the coin client.

7. Start your mining program by replacing the address you used to pool mine with http://127.0.0.1:y-u X –p Q

Step By Step Process Of Setting Up A Solo Server

STEP 1

On the start menu of the windows of your personal desktop, configure the startup script. Afterwards add the line flag-server. The RPC servers will be automatically turned on when the process is done. The RPC server enables direct communication with the miners.

STEP 2

In the personal installation user's directory, edit the Bitcoin.Conf file. In case you are a window's user, this will be located in the Users/xxx/AppData/Roaming/Bitcoin directory. The xxx stands for your user name from your PC. To find the app data, locate the local disk C, then select show hidden files; here the app data and other folders will be displayed. This file can be edited using: ultra-edit, notepad++, notepad or any other tool which keeps the file in text format.

It is not advisable to use Microsoft or WordPad in editing, as the file format is changed from their text format resulting to the Bitcoin-QT not able to recognize it. In the Bitcoin.conf file put the following:

Server=1

rpcuser=username

rpcpassword=password

rpcallowip=127.0.0.1

rpcport=8332

Use 127.0.0.1:8332 as the server and the username and the password of your choice as the credentials, to be able to connect CGMiner or BFGminer to Bitcoin-core client for mining to start. Mining from another computer means that you are not running client software on the same computer. Therefore, you will need to configure the parameter below

rpcallowip=192.168.1.110

Ensure that the IP address is that of the computer running the mining. While mining it is essential for your computer to not be using DHCP. This is because, in the event that there is a change in your IP address, mining will stop until you notice the problem and change it.

STEP 3

To set the solo mining server you will need to restart the server.

When it comes to solo mining, making profits can be very difficult, it takes a very long time for the profits to be released. This is because, gaining of a block can be very complicated.

Advantages Of Solo Mining

1. Solo mining does not incur any fees. This is because the discovered block, the transaction fees and 12.5 BTC are paid by the miner. You can get good earnings if you do merged mining plus ensuring that orphan rates are low. If you don't merged mine and have your orphan rate slip, the point turns to negative.

2. It has a higher uptime as it is less prone to outages.
3. Solo mining has a high variance. This is seen where once in a year you can get 25 BTC. In the case where you have fast hashpower you can be able to be paid monthly on average. In bad cases it can take 6 to 12 months.
4. It has a complicated setup for you are your own pool admin. The namecoind crashes often. The publically available pool software is broken, inefficient, no longer maintained or outdated. You need a good connectivity to the Bitcoin peer to peer network, in order to ensure that your blocks are not orphaned.
5. As a solo miner you are responsible for your own security this includes: softwareside security, dealing with ddos and the exploits attempts.
6. As a solo miner all the earned funds belongs to you as you do not have to share with anyone.

Disadvantages Of Solo Mining
1. Solo mining inclines to generating unpredictable income
2. Due to supporting getwork pull solo mining wastes time.
3. There is the need of purchasing expensive equipment, arrangement of the cooling system and its configuration.
4. It takes too long in calculating of one hash.

Pool Mining

Pool mining involves the pooling of resources together by miners. The miners share the processing power of a network plus splitting of the reward among themselves equally. The reward is split according to the work contributed by a miner to the probability of discovering a block.

Pool mining started when there was an increased difficulty in mining. It took years for a slower miner to be able to get a block, therefore, miners sort for a solution and came up with pool mining. Here they pool their resources in order to quickly generate blocks. The miners then receive a share of the block's reward consistently rather than once in few years.

Pool Mining Methods

In pool mining the hundreds and thousands of miners have a specialized protocol that they use. Here **B** represents a block reward minus the pool fee, **p** is the probability of finding a block in the share attempts and **D** stands for the current block difficulty. ($p=1/D$).

A pool is able to support a variable share difficulty. This means that as a miner you are able to select a share target and change the probability accordingly.

Payout Systems

Computing the shares you have earned in the Bitcoin is complex. As a result, a lot of computing schemes have been put in place. The following is a list of payment schemes.

1. Pay Per Share (PPS)

This is one of the most popular ways of payments. For the shifting of the risk to the mining pool plus guaranteeing you payment for the share you contribute. They require reserves of 10000 BTC so as to endure a streak of bad luck. The miners are able to withdraw their payout immediately.

2. Double Geometric Method (DGB)

This is a hybrid approach which allows the operator to take in some risk. The operator gets a portion of the payout in short rounds and is able to return the payout in longer rounds; hence, able to normalize the payments.

This is a general version of both PPLNS and Geometric methods, which involves new parameters. **o** (cross-round leakage), when o =O this is then a Geometric method. When o =1 it becomes a variant of PPLNS.

- Use parameters f, c and o.

- Initialize s = 1 when the pool starts to run. Let k be for every worker, therefore s_k is the worker' score then set $s_k = O$.
- Set r=1+1/c p (1-c) (1-0).if the parameter change then the r ought to be recalculated.
- Worker k submits a share, $S_k = S_k + (1-f)(1-c) spB$. S = sr
- In case of a valid block, give the worker k the following payout 1/cs (1-0) S_k. set $S_k = S_k.o$

3. Geometric Method

This method is based on the score as slush method. Here there is no advantage of either mining late or early.

- Select parameters f and c
- When starting a round set s = 1. For worker k let S_K be the score of the worker for the round then $S_K = o$
- Set r = 1 − p + p/c, here p =1/D. r needs to be updated if the difficulty changes.
- Worker k submits a share then set $S_K = S_k + spB$ and s =sr.

- End the round if the share is a valid block, pay worker k (1-f) (r-1) S_k divided by sp

4. Eligius

This method was designed in order to incorporate the PPS and BPM pools strength. To earn shares and get payouts immediately, miners submit proof of work. In distributing the block rewards, they are equally shared among miners with shares of the last valid block. Stale block shares are cycled to the next block's shares.

Miners are paid their rewards if they have earned a minimum amount of 67108864. In the case where the amount owed is lesser it is rolled over to the next block to achieve the limit amount required. If a share is not submitted by Bitcoin miner for over a week, the pool will then send the remaining balance irrespective of the size.

5. Triplemining

In this payout, medium-size pools that do not have fees and redistributes 1% of the block found are brought together. This allows your share to grow at a faster rate than any other pool mining. The admin of the Bitcoin pool mining adds the Bitcoin generated to a jackpot which is triggered. It is then paid to the pool member who found the block. This method allows all the members in a pool to be able to earn additional Bitcoin irrespective of their processing power.

Characteristics Of Pool Mining

1. It functions as a coordinator for the participants in a pool by:
   - taking hashes from the pool members.
   - Searching for block rewards
   - Assigning of the block rewards to members proportionally to their participation.
   - Recording all the work done by the participants.
2. The administrator of a pool ought to be exposed to Bitcoin network, plus listening to new blocks so as to be able to validate transactions.
3. The Bitcoin share is able to calculate the amount of work that a miner's hardware was able to do by going to the server. They then send the amount of Bitcoin.

4. Presence of a low pool fees plus a user-friendly interface.
5. Availability of additional functionality which has quickly links to other coin resources examples: official pages, news and exchanges among others. Take note they should be supportive and not dominating.

Using A Pool

When you have a pool to use, you need to set up an account then configure your miner to be able to log into the pool. There are two interfaces in the pool. The first interface is when mining software get the work and reports the results of work that is done. The second interface allows the user to be able to interact with the system. We are going to look at 50BTC and BTC mining pool.

50 BTC

50 BTC is named after the reward given when a block is found in the first 4 years. It has the lowest rates of PPS, this range from 2.5% to 3%. Transaction fees are

paid, although they have unreliable infrastructure, the payouts occur faster and they have a responsive support portal. The 50 BTC account provides you with:

- The current balance of your account
- A history of the difficulty
- A calculator which is very handy, for it is able to translate a hash rate amount to BTC or USD per day.
- A history of your mining effort
- The payout allows you to pay in different way, for instance liberty reserve.

BTC

It explains how to mine, where to get the software plus the details required to configure a miner. The site provides a clear explanation of their pay out for PPs and PPLNS. There is an easier mining effort leading to a lot of joining in.

The site has employed a 51% mitigation plan which reduces the likelihood of reaching 51% of the network. They continually raise the fee until people leave. This reduces the fees when the level are low enough, thus the community is not fearful of the pool reaching 51% of the network. The user interface is nicely polished plus easy to navigate.

Chapter 4: How To Set Up A Bitcoin Miner

Before setting up a Bitcoin miner it is important to understand what Bitcoin mining is. Bitcoin mining is running SHA256 double round hash: this is a verification process to be able to validate Bitcoin transaction. It also provides the necessary security to the public ledger of Bitcoin network. Bitcoin mining is legal and it's measured in hashes per second.

Bitcoin miners are compensated by Bitcoin networks for their efforts. This is done by releasing Bitcoin to miners who contribute the required computational power. The higher the computing power contribution by a miner the higher his/her share reward is.

Setting up a Bitcoin miner can be a complex task. It's also important to choose the hardware that you are going to use. When mining Bitcoin you will have Bitcoin transactions, this leads to other users being rewarded. This is the main mechanic that is behind the

Bitcoin economy. Mining keeps the transaction reliable and secure.

Step 1: Purchasing A Custom Mining Hardware

Desktop's CPU and GPU were used for Bitcoin mining, although this had to change due to the impractical returns. As a lot of electricity is used, yet the earnings from mining the coins are less compared to the expense incurred in mining. Therefore, custom hardware was adopted as it has a better processing for the same power draw.

Custom hardware is in cards form and is inserted into the computer the same way a graphic card is inserted. Butterfly labs, CoinTerra and Bitcoin Ultra are some of the popular Bitcoin-hardware brands that are used. A Bitcoin mining machine price is dependent on the number of operations it's able to complete in a second.

In older days it was possible to use your computer CPU or a high speed video processor card to mine. Today this is no longer possible, you can use custom Bitcoin ASIC chips; they have a performance of up to 100x capability of the previous systems. It is important to mine Bitcoin using the best Bitcoin mining hardware that is designed specifically for mining.

When deciding on the hardware to use considers the hash rate and the energy consumption. Hash rate are the number of calculations, your hardware is able to perform in a second; so as to solve the mathematical problem in the mining section. It's measured in megahashes, gigahashes and terahashes per second. When you have a hardware with the highest hash rate, it is considered as the best in solving the transaction in finding a block.

Mining of Bitcoin involves computing which utilizes a lot of electricity, when making your choice consider your hardware energy utilization in watts. Ensure that you do not spend a lot of money on electricity used in mining coins, which is not equivalent to the reward paid for finding a block. Know how many hashes you get for every watt of electricity used. This is done by dividing the hash count by the number of watts utilized.

When it comes to hardware, there are three main categories to pick from: the ASICs, GPUs and FPGAs. The CPU is the least powerful category of your Bitcoin mining hardware. This can be improved by adding GPUs, which are designed to compute heavy mathematical lifting; therefore, able to calculate the complex polygons.

Field Programmable Gate Array (FPGA) is a circuit integrated to configure after it's built in. It enables the buying of chips in large volume, customizing them for Bitcoin mining before putting them in their equipment. ASICs on the other hand are made to do a particular thing, to mine Bitcoin at a mind-crushing speed using low power consumption. ASICs allow the use of specific Bitcoin mining hardware.

Reasons Why Custom Hardware Is Preferred
1) The Bitcoin mining hardware is readily available. They include: CoinTerra, Butterfly Labs and Bitcoin Ultra among others.
2) Presence of Bitcoin mining machines which is very affordable. Their cost is dependent on their hash rate and the rate at which they can complete a calculation in seconds.
3) It has a faster and better processing speed.

4) Custom hardware can be easily inserted into a computer; this is due to graphic card like appearance.

Step 2: Obtaining A Bitcoin Wallet

Bitcoin earned are stored in digital wallets which are encrypted in order to protect your money. The wallets can either be online or local. Online wallets cannot be accessed by your online services, but the wallets are considered to be disastrous in the vent that something happens on their end.

Local wallet are a preference to most Bitcoin users, this is because of security reasons. They involve verifying of the entire blockchain. This is the history of all the Bitcoin transactions. Bitcoin is kept running and secure by hosting the blockchain; when you syncing the blockchain for the first time, it can take a whole day or even more.

Wallet apps for your mobile phone are also available. They do not necessitate downloading of an entire blockchain. The apps include: CoinJar and Blockchain. Some of the local wallet includes: Multibit (does not require downloading an entire blockchain), BitcoinQT and Armory. In the event that you lose your wallet you will also lose your money.

When you have your wallet ensure that you have an address for it; which is a long sequence of numbers and letters. It is important to note that you will require a public Bitcoin address not your password, which is the private key. Copay is good Bitcoin wallet; it is able to function on different operating systems. You can also use a Bitcoin hardware wallet.

Step 3: Secure Your Wallet

When it comes to wallet there is no ownership. This is because, anyone who is able to access the wallet is able to do with the coins as they like. To avoid this authorize a two-factor authentication. This is done by storing your wallet on a computer with no internet access.

You can also store the wallet on a SD card and have it on the go. It's important to have a copy of the wallet.dat file on your thumb drive, print a copy and store it in safe location. This prevents you from losing your coins in case the computer crashes and you do not have a copy of the wallet.dat file.

Step 4: Decide The Mining Pool To Join Or Whether To Mine Alone

When it comes to mining coins, as a miner you have two options to either start mining alone or join an established pool. When you are mining alone it can be difficult to get a new Bitcoin, for they are very competitive though you are able to keep all that you mine. In pool mining you share the resources plus split rewards, this results to quicker returns.

If you are solo mining, you can end up going for a year or so without earning a Bitcoin. Yet for pool mining this is not possible as the coin is given to the pool that discovered it. A majority of pools have a lower rate of around 2% fee of your earnings.

In case you are in pool mining you will have to create a worker. This is an account which is used to monitor your contributions to the pool. It is possible to have multiple workers in an account, pools have specific instructions in creating workers; have a workers ID to enable the pool to keep track of your contributions. When choosing which pool mining to join consider the following:

- What is their reward method?
- What is their fee for mining plus when withdrawing the funds?
- How frequent does the pool find a reward?
- How stable is the pool?
- How easy is it to withdraw funds from the pool?

Step 5: Download A Mining Program

Depending on the hardware that you are using, there are different mining programs that you can use. You will find your mining program running in the command line; you may require a batch file for it to start correctly. This is especially in the case that you are using pool mining.

CGminer and BFGminer are the most popular mining programs. Easyminer is another program which runs on graphical interface instead of a command line. You can check your pool's help guide when you are connecting to your mining program.

If you are solo mining make sure to connect your mining program to your personal wallet. This will ensure that whatever you earn is automatically deposited into the wallet. If you are pool mining connect your user account with your wallet, so that the coins can be transferred.

Step 6: Run Your Miner

After configuring your miner, you can know start mining. If needed run your batch file, the miner will connect and start to mine. As the miner works the rest of your computer will most likely slow to a crawl. Depending on the pool of your choice, your payment will be determined by the share of coins you have. Therefore, ensure that you enter your address in the fields while signing into a pool.

Step 7: Keep An Eye On The Temperatures

While you are mining the mining programs push the hardware to their limits, this is especially in the case where the hardware was not intended for mining. You can use programs like the SpeedFan which are designed to prevent temperatures from going above the safe limits. For instance, graphics cards are not to go above 80^0c.

Step 8: Check Your Profitability

After mining for some time, it is important to check your figures in order for you to know whether or not it's worth mining. Compare the amount you get with the expenses you incur while mining. How much money did you spend in keeping your computer running? Use parameters like hash rate, equipment cost, and current Bitcoin price and power consumption for you to see the time you will take to be able pay back your investments.

Network difficulty is one of the key parameters. How hard it is to solve a transaction block is determined by this metric. It varies according to the hash rate of the network. As ASIC devices come into the market, difficulty increases. Therefore, increase the metric in the calculator which will enable you to know your investments when more people are joining the market.

Chapter 5: The Network Of Bitcoin

Bitcoin works through peer to peer transaction. This network is created while transferring Bitcoins from one person to another. Every transaction, however, depends on the specific features of the model being used by the two peers. For every Bitcoin networking model to be effective, each peer must provide a destination of the participant. The Internet is the key factor running the entire transaction. Why is the transaction is referred to us peer to peer transaction? Well, the reason here is that there is uniformity for the networking computers participating in the transaction. This means that the two devices are similar in all aspects, with equal nodes that play a role in network services provider. The special thing with these nodes sharing the network is that they function on a flat topology; a mesh network controlling all the activities of the transaction. Therefore, performance is on equal chances with no participant on top of the other. The services are never centralized, and there is no server for central monitoring of the transaction. Networking, therefore, ensures transparency of the transaction and a mandate for each participant to exercise full control over the entire transaction. The sharing nodes make this possible. During a peer to peer transaction, the networking nodes for both the participants will produce and consume services simultaneously. Participation Incentives are earned as reciprocal of the undertaking.

Features Of The Peer To Peer Network

The major feature of the peer to peer transaction networks is that they are decentralized. This is the control factor of the Bitcoin industries, making the entire process remain on flat topology level. No hierarchy of participation, in that no one is on the top of the other, but instead, everything is taking place at the same level. Additionally, peer to peer transactions networks are open and inherently resilient. Some years back the peer to peer networking worked on a pre-eminent network of the early internet architecture, with equal computer networking nodes. Today, though the topology of the internet protocol is on the same level, the architecture of the internet has been modified to be a bit hierarchical.

Bitcoin Peer To Peer Network And Protocols

Bitcoin network can be defined as a group of network sharing nodes that run the peer to peer transaction of the Bitcoin. Bitcoin network involves other protocols being bridged by the gateway routers to the major Bitcoin protocol. Example of the intermediate protocol is the stratum protocol. These are networking protocols for the mobile, and lightweight wallets, as well as the protocols, used when mining. How does the stratum protocol get to the major Bitcoin protocol? Just as mentioned earlier, stratum protocol is an intermediary connecting other activities to the major peer to peer Bitcoin network. Through the peer to peer Bitcoin protocol, the router servers are able to reach the Bitcoin network. This provides a network extension to the sharing nodes in order to run the network to the other protocols. For instance, the mining nodes of a stratum are connected via a routing server to its protocol, which then connects the protocol to the major Bitcoin network and finally it is bridged to the peer to peer Bitcoin transaction protocol. A Bitcoin system is, therefore, an extended network connecting the overall transaction network; the P2P Bitcoin transacting protocols and the subset blockchain protocols such as the stratum and the pool mining protocols.

Besides being decentralized, Bitcoin networking is beyond being a flat topology. Well, you could need a simple reminder of Bitcoin to understand well what flat topology network is all about. To be simple and precise Bitcoin is a digital peer to peer designed cryptocurrency system. More so the network architecture for the transaction is founded on the reflection of the latter. Enhancing a decentralized system is the main focus in Bitcoin networking. It is designed to enhance a flat topology and to avoid centralized networking consensus.

Networking Nodes And Their Functions

Bitcoin cryptocurrency networking nodes refers to a package of functions of a Bitcoin network. These include: mining, routing, providing wallet services as well as provision of a blockchain database. Not forgetting that the Bitcoin peer to peer network is decentralized and that they function on a flat topology, the network nodes, however, tend to assume different functions based on their supportive roles. Therefore every network covers a full node of functionality. This full node is made of four features which are: a wallet, network routing node, a miner and the full blockchain database. Apart from route network functions, the nodes may include other different functions. Generally, the network nodes will assist in propagating and validation of both the blocks and the transactions. The nodes will also function by discovering peer to peer connections and maintaining the connections. Peer to peer connections is dependent on the blockchain, and it should always be updated. A full node will, therefore, ensure that the blockchain is complete and updated regularly. Moreover, the full nodes will help in maintaining a decentralized functionality of the cryptocurrency Bitcoin network by conducting an independent autonomous and authoritative verification.

Simplified Payment Verification Nodes (Spv) And Lightweight Nodes

The simplified payment verification nodes and the light nodes are minor protocol nodes. These simple nodes play a great role in controlling the functioning of a single subset of the entire blockchain. SPV will thereafter verify the payment of such transaction. Normally, to differentiate the full node and simple nodes, the full blockchain for the full node functioning database is circled with different colors and indicated full blockchain. The lightweight nodes and the simplified verification nodes have different colors drawings to distinguish from the latter and an indication that they only have a subset copy of the full blockchain.

The Mining Nodes

The function of the mining nodes is to create brand new Bitcoin blocks. The networking nodes work with the aid of hardware which when run will compute the maths and build Bitcoin blocks through the display of a proof of work algorithm. Mining nodes are made of lightweight nodes for a subset copy of the blockchain and a full node with a complete up to date copy of the entire blockchain. Lightweight nodes function mostly in pool mining and use router server to connect them to the main Bitcoin full node.

Wallet

Many refer to it as the user wallet since it contains the user's destination address. Example of the user wallet is the mobile smartphones among other devices such as the laptops and the desktops. A user wallet may display full node or lightweight node functionality. Most interesting to note is that similar to the many clients participating through desktops user wallets will mainly display a full node networking. Most of the user wallets with lightweight and simplified payments verification nodes are those that use such devices as mobile and smartphones. This is because they strain their resources a lot as compared to other devices. The protocols subsidiary to the main Bitcoin peer to peer transaction protocols are run by the servers and lightweight nodes. Such networking nodes are the lightweight protocols for client access and the mining pools special protocols. Therefore, note that the Bitcoin network for extended networking contains the following types of nodes and their functions.

Bitcoin Core

This is the reference client network which contains the user wallet, node for network routing server, full blockchain database and the miner necessary for peer to peer Bitcoin network.

Full Blockchain Node

The full blockchain node for Bitcoin peer to peer network is made of the network router node and a database full blockchain.

Solo Miner

The solo miner is made of the full up to date blockchain copy, mining functions and Bitcoin peer to peer network routing node.

Lightweight wallet (SPV)

This may not contain the full node blockchain database but has the network routing node on the peer to peer Bitcoin network and a user wallet.

Pool Protocol Servers

These are the gateway routers connecting the major Bitcoin protocol to the other protocols. i.e. they offer connectivity of Bitcoin peer to peer network to the rest of the nodes running other protocols. These include the stratum and the pool mining nodes.

Understanding Extended Bitcoin Network

An extended network consists of the network running the main peer to peer Bitcoin protocol and different nodes used in running various protocols. The lightweight nodes also known as the simplified verification nodes are joined to the peer to peer main Bitcoin network. These are the pool route servers and the gateways for the subsidiary protocols. Others include pool mining protocol nodes, the lightweight user wallet client protocols among other protocols without a full copy of database blockchain.

According to the full node Bitcoin network, a maximum of 10000 nodes and a minimum of 7000 nodes are necessary in order to run peer to peer Bitcoin protocol among other versions of the Bitcoin core or references. The BitcoinJ, btcd and the Libbitcoin add up to few less than hundred nodes implementing various auxiliary peer to peer transaction Bitcoin protocols. Other mining nodes represent an insignificant percentage of the main peer to peer transaction Bitcoin network. Both offer stiff competition invalidating of the mining process and transactions, ensuring verifications and creating of brand new Bitcoin blocks. Most of the large companies operating Bitcoin peer to peer transaction network run full node Bitcoin references. These contain a full up to date blockchain copies and a main Bitcoin network node. However, this does not contain the user wallet functions or the mining details. Except other nodes, the nodes for the interface of the large companies are also referred as the edge router network. These give room for the other services such as the processing of the merchant payments, making exchanges, block exploring and verification of the user wallets.

Network Transactions

Bitcoin transactions revolve along networking from the individuals. Every transaction is different depending on the networking model. Various transactions outline the peer addresses indicating the transaction source as well as its destinations. For a single transaction, there is two destinations and more than one addresses. Your peer partner to where you are transferring your Bitcoins becomes your first destination. The second destination represents the user wallet addresses, while the third destination is not determined by either of the two peers. It represents the address of the intermediary arising in the transaction especially when the destinations of the two transacting peers did not add up. This could be the scenario introducing the third destinations. Ann and Isaac are carried out a Bitcoin transaction where Ann sent 100 Bitcoins to Isaac. For this case, Isaac address is our first destination while Ann's user wallet address where the 100 Bitcoins are being charged represents the second destination. A situation may arise where martins address shares the same wallet with ann. in such a circumstance, the three destination will contain the following Bitcoins in their addresses: Ann address 150 Bitcoins, Isaac address 100 Bitcoins and martins address 49.5 Bitcoins. The missing 0.5 Bitcoins represents transaction fee payment to the miners. Once the mining activity is over, it is encrypted for network submission and continuity of the next step which is confirmation. This occurs when the network takes the encrypted transaction and it is added to the already existing block. It is only after the transaction has been fully encrypted in the current block chain when Isaac is able to claim the 100 Bitcoins sent by Ann as his own.

Bitcoin-QT is the software installed in the device of the peers. With it, the user wallet is safe and secure on their devices. The software moreover creates a peer to peer network node that helps in blockchain distribution. This node signals a working command hence mining starts once the node is used to register a miner. The two peers can now request to start mining. The lottery won during mining help in boosting the processing power of the network. After every mining activity, the miners get hash as a form of payment.

Exploring Bitcoin Networking Blocks

As discussed earlier, it is clear that after every mining activity a hash is produced. In case the hash produced as a lower value compared to the block found previously, then, a new Bitcoin block has been discovered which should then be passed for submission and verification. The P2P network has also to confirm the newfound block to allow for the closing of the old block and opening of the newly discovered block. After that the founder of the block is awarded. Well, a transaction shall be considered confirmed in case the P2P network has attained a total of six transactions confirms achieved by the creation of new blocks. Confirmation plays a vital role in ensuring that double spending does not occur during a transaction. The maximum numbers of the bit-coins in the Bitcoin industry are 21,000,000 BTC. After every transaction, the reward has halved a technique used to ensure that the Bitcoin value keeps on increasing. Therefore, even with the most insignificant Bitcoin reward, it is sufficient enough compared to the government currency hence participants will always be attracted to the market. Currently, one Bitcoin is worth $200, hence with 10BTC is equivalent to $2000. Each day, a system releases a fixed amount of Bitcoins.

Bitcoin Difficulty Networking Factor

The ease at which the P2P network finds a new block is controlled by a factor referred to us as difficulty. The level of difficulty is changed after every 14 days or every time 2,016 blocks are created. To determine the processing power of a system is done by calculating hash rate or hashes produced in every second. Hash can, therefore, be defined as taking computer algorithms inputs, carrying out math computations on the same and coming up with a long string representing it. Bitcoin uses SHA 256 hash, a notation of Hex-Decimal representation with 64 characters ranging between A-F or could be 0-9. Use of hashes in the Bitcoin industry is important as its verification is less complicated and it's impossible to reverse the payments when using it. Currently, hash rate is measured using TH/s. You will, therefore, encounter such mining units as Hashes per second: H/S, Kilo Hashes per second (KH/s), Mega Hashes per second (MH/s) and Giga Hashes per second (GH/s) and Tera Hashes per second

(TH/s) and Peta Hashes per second (PH/s). These measures of units relate as follows.

1,000 H/s = 1 KH/s

1,000 KH/s = 1 MH/s

1,000 MH/s = 1 GH/s

1,000 GH/s = 1 TH/s

1000 TH/s = 1 PH/s.

Networking Through Pool Mining Or Solo Mining

A miner can either carry out solo or pool mining. Whereby solo mining means individual based mining in which the miner will connect his/her device to their networking node, and in case they create a block, they receive a reward. On the other hand, pool mining involves a group of miners mining together, who share the reward by splitting it equally in case they find a block. Whether a miner in a group of pool found or did not find the block, they still stand a chance of being paid in relation to the contribution they offered. Example, Ann, and Isaac have the same hash Power of 2.1 GH, and they get indulged in pool mining each earning 40 BTC for the contributed efforts. Isaac did not find any block while Ann was able to find three. One of the blocks Ann found was 50 BTC and the other two blocks were 25 BTC each. In such a situation Ann will only receive 40 BTC while the rest 100 BTC are taken to the pool. Unlike for the case of pool mining Ann would be rewarded for the blocks, she found it was Solo mining. Moreover, if Ann found the block in the pool, the poo operate receives the reward for such a discovered block. Ann will also benefit from finding the block as each transaction for each founded block is included in her block if she was solo mining. However, the pool operator will instead earn the fee in case she was involved in pool mining.

Chapter 6: Strategies To Use In Mining And Trading Bitcoin

Strategies To Use In Mining Bitcoin

When it comes to mining Bitcoin, we want to get the best profit there is with the least amount of expenses incurred. As a result, we need to have strategies to make this possible. In order for you to be successful in Bitcoin mining you need to have a well thought out strategy. The following is a list of strategies to consider.

1. Purchase The Most Efficient Miner

In today's Bitcoin mining, Application-Specific Integrated Circuit (ASIC) has completely taken over. ASIC machines are able to mine at exceptional speed, consuming less power compared to FPGA or the GPU mining hardware. The best Bitcoin mining hardware is determined by its price per hash and the electric efficiency, the options include: Avalon, AntMiner S7 and AntMiner S9.

ASIC chips are Bitcoin mining hardware that is designed specifically for mining Bitcoin blocks. They are able to solve Bitcoin blocks and in the process using less power compared to, the older Bitcoin mining hardware such as: FPGAs and the GPUs. Bitcoin mining is becoming more popular, consequently making the price of Bitcoin rise plus the value of getting an ASIC Bitcoin mining hardware.

When purchasing an ASIC miner consider its hash rate, efficiency and the price. What is its hash rate? This is important because the more the hashes the more it costs, therefore, making efficiency very important. Get a miner that has a high efficiency, for you need a miner that is able to convert your amount of electricity to Bitcoin

When it comes to price, the efficient and fastest mining hardware has a higher price. Bitcoin Mining hardware which is cheap in price tends to mine lesser Bitcoin. When purchasing a miner do not look at the price and the hash rate only, but check its efficiency also. This means always aim at the value of the miner.

2. Management Of Your Difficulty And Power

Difficulty is known as the measure of how difficult it is for an individual to be able to find hash below a certain target. For Bitcoin network there is a global block difficulty. Difficulty _1_target is the formula of a difficulty.

In Bitcoin mining power used is very essential. As a miner, you do not want to spend a lot of money paying for electricity. Yet the block you mined is not worth the amount of money spent in mining it. The amount of power used in order to generate a block at a mean of 10 minutes is known as hash power.

Difficulty and hash power are dependent on each other. This is seen when a Bitcoin's network difficulty increases, the hash power required to find a block will also increase. The Bitcoin's difficulty increases because of the many miners joining the network, hence, the increase in the hash power.

The best strategy that you can have for Bitcoin mining is keeping your costs low. You can do this by ensuring the power (electricity) you use and the Bitcoin miner's costs are low. Having these in control will enable you to get good revenue from mining Bitcoin.

3. Choose A Mining Pool

When you have your hardware set and you are ready to go, you need to decide if you are going to mine alone or join a pool which has collective miners. Mining alone means that you would need to incur all the expenses, but on a brighter side, you will have all the rewards obtained from getting a block. Solo mining requires you to have high hashing power for you to find a block. In the event that your hashing power is low, you can end up mining for months to even years without having to earn a single Bitcoin.

As a miner in a pool, this means that you are able to earn regular rewards even if they are small. The amount of reward is based on your contribution to the pool. As a member of a pool you will have a fee that you are required to pay. In this strategy ensure that you choose an established low-fee pool to join.

4. Consider Your Infrastructure

When it comes to the infrastructure in mining, these are all the things needed to get Bitcoin miners connected and working. Having a bit of data networking information will be helpful. You can easily get this in Cisco CCNA certification guide. Consider the following in infrastructure:

5. The Firewall And Router

Internet connection is needed for the miners to be able to download hashing puzzle and to upload the solutions in order to earn money. The internet connection does not have to be fast as long as it's reliable. Have a firewall that has a remote access that is VPN capable. This will allow you to remotely access the equipment.

6. Power Distribution Unit

Have the bunch of 220 VAC, 30 Amp connections. On each Antminer use 6Amps of 220VAC power, this means 30 amp of power distribution will be possible, therefore 4 Antminers can be powered.

7. Power Cords

You need power cables that connect the supply power and the power distribution unit. You will require IEC C14 to C13.

8. Network Switches

Every Bitcoin miner has a separate network connection. You require a network switch for it to work, plus the switches does not need to be fast.

Strategies To Use In Trading Bitcoin

When it comes to trading, Bitcoin is a superior instrument compared to Forex or commodities and stocks. This is because Bitcoin trades for 24 hours for all the 7 days in a week. For stocks and commodities they trade only during the office hours and not to forget for Forex, during the weekends their markets are shut.

Bitcoin is also the cheapest, most convenient and quickest instrument for trading. When it comes to fees they have a minimal charge compared to other exchanges. Bitcoin withdrawals or their deposit are done within hours worldwide. Bitcoin also has exceptional unpredictability which allows percentage profit without leverage.

In order to ensure that you make the most out of Bitcoin trading, you need to understand what Bitcoin mining is and how it works. Also know the strategies that you can use in order to maximize your profits. The following is a list of strategies you can follow so as to ensure you get high returns.

Buy And Hold

Within the Bitcoin community these traders are known as holders. These holders utilize the long-term approach in Bitcoin as a result, benefit on the rising price of Bitcoin. Here the trader main goal is to get as much Bitcoin as possible, for they were able to foresee it becoming valuable with time.

Buy and hold strategy is very common in trading Bitcoin, it requires one to base their actions on the different fundamental analysis rather than on technical analysis. Decisions are made on the potential of the Bitcoin and not on the current charts and trends. A daily change of the Bitcoin price does not move the holders although they are bothered by the fluctuations.

In this strategy price crashes are viewed as major opportunities for them to buy more Bitcoin. This will lead to a lot of revenue in the long run. Price crash is considered as discount that needs to be capitalized on. If prices reach a peak, profits are pulled but you do not liquidate all your Bitcoin assets.

Trend Trading

The trend trading strategy is a bit hard to navigate compared to other strategies. Here as a trader you enter into prolong patterns with an aim of capitalizing on it all the way to the end of the trend. The traders do not have a specific target in mind.

Trends grow when people rush towards them. As they gain momentum and are strong, they are able to be noticed by non-Bitcoin owners plus the media. Therefore, this draws more attention to the trend with time.

The prices will go up and start to extend drastically. At this stage the trend will start to crash at an alarming rate. Here quality trend traders will get in quick, make money and exit before the crash hits everyone.

Swing Trading

The strategy here is to be able to trade with a significant price, while moving between the two different extremes. Traders here hold for a few days or months. For instance, when the price is not following either a strong upward or downward trend it will fall in between the high and low cost.

Buyers or seller enter the market when the market is linked with volume. This will result in a fixed price reverse in direction. Swing traders also rely on technical indicators which reveal overbought or oversold conditions on the market.

Traders can bet on the reversal of price once the Bitcoin reach a certain level. This is possible when the indicators are based on direction or a change. If the prices are not reversed back, this is a clear indication of time to leave the trade.

Scalping

When it comes to scalping it involves individuals who want to profit on the minute by minute exchanges. Different imbalances are used to book and order a collection of the minor profits. This strategy allows individuals to get massive returns through volume of the smaller profits.

In scalping it is more about the volume of trades rather than the size of the trades. The chart used by scalpers shows a 5 minutes time in duration. This kind of trading is tough and requires the trader to have a lot of experience.

Day Trading

This strategy requires people who know how to maintain their position in a market while they are on duty. They can operate a shift of 12 to 16 hours in the least. The traders are able to change from swing to day trading; they can also keep certain accounts until it's time to liquidate them. It's possible to trade on trends and scalp if needed.

With day trading you can follow sub-hourly or hourly charts with an occasional reference to the higher time frames. The strategy involves individuals who want to make Bitcoin trading their fulltime occupation but not a part time hustle.

Leverage is another Bitcoin trading strategy, although using leverage is risky. Keep this in mind especially if you are thinking of opening a big position in the market. Due to its nature Bitcoin has become a special instrument in trading.

Other strategy in Bitcoin trading includes: understanding all essential risks that are present, study the charts in order to find trends, set limit orders and be very patient, once you have bought and sold some Bitcoin, graduate to the big leagues such as the Global Digital Asset Exchange (GDAX). Another good strategy is reading the Bitcoin news on daily basis, here you can find websites to bookmark for discussion boards or Bitcoin news. These are just some of the strategies you can consider while Bitcoin trading.

Conclusion

Similar to the money market, the Bitcoin pricing may inflate or deflate with time. Though mostly, the price is moving upwards, it is important to keenly note that as time it goes down. Today, a Bitcoin is over $2100 while a year back it was $ 150. Changes are expected any time hence readiness is very necessary. With the current trend in the Bitcoin industry, it is expected that the value of Bitcoin will maintain the upward curve for some while though it may assume a low curve anytime soon. In fact, since the industry is growing and getting new updates, there are high expectations that in the near future the Bitcoin providers will change their service provision rules. These may include: hiking the price, stopping confirmations or increasing charging fees.

Once you transact with Bitcoins, it is not possible to do a reverse, unless your transacting partner reversed it for you. Unlike the debit and the credit cards such as the PayPal and the master cards, there is no central agency to file a claim in case you lose your Bitcoins, hence when you make your payments, make sure you double check the Bitcoin key address for confirmation.